CREEPY CRAWLIES

INFESTING RODENTS

By Rachel Eagen

Published in 2013 by Dalmatian Press, LLC, Franklin, TN 37068-2068.
1-866-418-2572. DalmatianPress.com

CE16314/1012
Printed in China

Developed and produced by Plan B Book Packagers,
Editorial director: Ellen Rodger, **Art director:** Rosie
Gowsell-Pattison, **Editor:** Molly Aloian,
Project manager: Kathy Middleton

Photographs: Istockphoto: p. 10; BremecR: p. 16; Engraving by Gustave Dore, Photo by D Walker: p. 9; Don Kurto: p. 21(top); Peregrina: p. 14 (top); Shutterstock: cover, p. 1; AJancso: p. 5; Ammit: p. 11 (top); Zvonimir Atletic: p. 7 (bottom); Bliznetsov: p. 2; Sergey Chirkov: p. 3 (bottom); Christopher Futcher: p. 23 (top); Four Oaks: p. 22 (bottom right); Igor Golovniov: p. 17; M van der Grond: p. 6; Eric Isselee: p. 14 (bottom); Cathy Keifer: p. 24 (bottom); Oleg Kozlov: p. 22 (top); Philip Lange: p. 23 (bottom); Iculig: p. 11 (bottom), 19; Lisovskaya Natalia: p. 13 (top); Lowe Llaguno: p. 8 (top); Male Witch: p. 3 (top); Maslov Dimitry: p. 4, 7 (top), 8 (bottom left), 17 (bottom); Ragnarock: p. 8 (bottom right), 12, 22 (top right); Shcherbakov Ilya: p. 13 (bottom), 21 (bottom); turtleman: p. 20; Utekhina Anna: p. 18; Zdorov Kirill Vladimirovich: p. 1, 10; VR Photos: p. 24 (top); Olga Zakrevska: p. 22 (bottom left)

S0-CFQ-642

scratch and sniff

What is buck-toothed, shortsighted, and furry? Who are the midnight bandits that rifle through the garbage and dart away at the sound of footsteps? The answer to both of these questions is: RATS. They live on almost every continent, happily nesting in dumpsters, riverbanks, and the walls of buildings. Rats can adapt, survive, and thrive in almost any environment and against all odds.

It's a Rat's Life

Loved and hated the world over, rats outnumber humans on every continent except Antarctica. They devour human food, spread disease, and wreak havoc on natural environments. They chew through wood, metal, bone, and even electrical wires—accidentally setting houses on fire. Rats contaminate huge stores of grain with their urine and droppings, making it unfit for humans to eat. Rats are also to blame for thousands of cases of food poisoning and other illnesses.

Rats live almost everywhere, including your neighborhood.

Foe and Friend

Luckily, rats are not all bad. Curious, affectionate, and smart, they are beloved pets in many families. Rats also help save lives. They are used in labs for research on human diseases such as cancer. Scientists test medicines on rats to ensure that they are safe enough for people to use. The reason why rats make such excellent test subjects is that their internal organs, such as their hearts, brains, and kidneys, work in a lot of the same ways that human organs do. Currently, rats are even helping scientists to learn more about spinal cord injuries. One day, this work might allow people in wheelchairs to walk again.

crawly fact

Nothing but the Tooth

Rats have chisel-like front teeth that are visible from the outside, when their mouths are closed. Unlike human teeth, rats' pearly whites grow constantly—up to five inches (12.7 cm) every year! So how do rats keep their teeth the same length? By chewing! Rats can gnaw through just about any material, including wood, plastic, and metal. They can easily dig through cinder blocks, gently hacking their way through newly constructed buildings. Their teeth are so strong that they can chomp down with a force of 24,000 pounds (10,886 kg) per square inch—that's more than 20 times the strength of the human bite.

Pet rats are gentle.

creepy stuff

Thanks for the Grub

Rats are commensal, a word that comes from two Latin words: *con mensa*, which means *to share a table*. Certain species of rats became dependent on humans hundreds of years ago, and they have never looked back. Quite simply, these rats need people. In North America, there are only two main types of commensal rats: Norway and black rats.

It is thanks to humans that commensal rats have become the most widely distributed mammals on Earth. Rats live everywhere people do. The reason? The food! Rats scavenge human food and squat in human shelters. Rats live under the porch, in the attic, and behind the walls of buildings. They scurry through the subways and take up residence in restaurants.

Don't mind if I do... Rats are house guests even when they are not pets.

Stuffed with Rats

Here is a question that has befuddled scientists for centuries: Just how many rats are there? At one time, it was thought that in cities, there was probably about one rat for every person. But with huge populations like New York City (over 8.3 million), scientists went back to check their numbers. Today, it is believed that rats outnumber humans worldwide, but it is still difficult to say how many live in one place. Some scientists believe that in big cities, where food and shelter are readily available, it is safe to say that there is at least one rat per 36 people.

That's creepy

As a densely populated city near a body of water, New York City is practically a resort for rats.

Today's Special: Roasted Rat

When explorers first began sailing the seas in search of new lands, it was not uncommon for sailors to dine on rats. Ships were not equipped with modern refrigeration, so food spoiled very quickly. Rats, always plentiful on ships, became a reliable meal. Today, these protein-packed rodents are enjoyed in many parts of the world, including the Philippines, Vietnam, China, and parts of East Africa. In Sicily, it is not uncommon to find rats in markets, sold in bundles tied together by their tails.

Germ Carriers

Rats have been accused of spreading deadly diseases for centuries. Rats tend to live in crowded, filthy conditions, making them excellent carriers of food poisoning. But it gets worse. Rats can also spread leptospirosis (also known as Weil's disease), typhus, spotted fever, trichinosis, rat-bite fever, and hanta virus.

5

Rat History

Rats started scurrying around about 65 million years ago, as the dinosaurs began to die out. Over time, they grew smaller and adapted to virtually every environment, attaching themselves to humans about 10,000 years ago. Since then, rats have become one of the most successful and numerous mammals on the planet.

The First Rats

Rats belong to a family of animals called Muridae. Millions of years ago, Muridae animals burrowed through the landscape of present-day Pakistan and Afghanistan. These animals adapted and developed different characteristics, resulting in over 500 different species. One of these species, Karnimata, evolved in Southeast Asia about 3.5 million years ago, eventually becoming an entirely different species: Rattus.

Rattus rattus

The first rats lived without the help of humans. They dug homes into riverbanks, swam through swamps, and fished in rivers. On the Indian subcontinent—a region that includes present-day Pakistan, India, Bangladesh, Nepal, Tibet, and Bhutan— these rats grew larger, darker, and developed long, naked tails to help them climb through thick forests. They reproduced quickly and in great numbers, and lived in groups known as colonies. This *Rattus rattus* species is more commonly known today as the black, ship, or roof rat.

cool climate

Rattus rattus did not stay put. They spread north, arriving in the cooler climate of northeastern China and as far north as present-day Siberia. These rats grew bigger, furrier, and stronger. Only slightly longer but twice the weight, the species is now known as *Rattus norvegicus*, or the Norway rat. Other common names for this species are the brown, wharf, and sewer rat. The name of this species is a little confusing, because these rats are rarely brown, but tawny, gray, creamy, white, black, blonde, albino, and ginger in color.

Hitching a Ride

Rats soon learned the advantages of living with humans. Not only did humans supply rats with an endless supply of food waste, they also provided shelter.

Rats tunneled under human dwellings and set up camp. Before long, rats and humans were inseparable— where people went, rats followed. Beginning in 1063, European Christians launched a series of military campaigns to gain control of present-day Israel and Palestine. These campaigns lasted about 200 years. Armies traveled between Europe and the Middle East. Black rats hitched a ride with these travelers and arrived in Europe.

Many rats came to Europe from the Holy Land during a series of military campaigns called the Crusades.

7

Stowaways

Rats really started getting around when trade opened up between Asia and Europe. Beginning in the 1300s, Europeans began searching the markets of Asia for silk, spices, and tea. They arrived in huge ships and left heavy with cargo. Norway rats were hiding in the overloaded holds of the ships when they set sail. The rats quickly got comfortable in Europe and spread out as Europeans colonized North and South America.

Outnumbered

While black rats were the first Rattus species, they were unable to hold their own when Norway rats arrived in Europe and North America. The Norway cousins are simply stronger and more powerful. Their extra bulk makes them especially suited to colder regions of northern climates. Over time, Norway rats outnumbered black rats in both Europe and North America. Today, black rats are found in the warmer climates of South America and Africa, as well as in the palm trees of southern California.

Rats sometimes nest in palm trees like these in California.

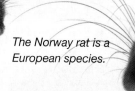

The Norway rat is a European species.

Black Death

In the mid-1300s, a terrible disease swept through Asia and Europe, killing millions of people. Victims suffered horribly for four or five days, and were usually dead within a week. Symptoms included high fever, chills, and painful lumps in the groin, armpits, and neck. These lumps, called buboes, filled with blood, eventually turning black as the victim died. This disease became known as the bubonic plague, or the Black Death.

Fear and Panic

No one understood the disease at the time. They only knew that plague victims suffered terribly before finally dying. It was not until 1894 that scientists finally knew where to cast the blame: fleas. The rat flea, *Xenopsylla cheopis*, which clings to a rat's fur, feeds on an infected rat and picks up the plague bacteria, *Yersinia pestis*. The bacteria are transferred to human victims when the fleas dine on human blood, their second-favorite meal.

Fleas carried by rats spread the Yersinia pestis bacteria, which caused the bubonic plague. Millions of people died from the plague.

crawly fact

Rat baiting

In the late 1800s, rats were used for sport in Europe and the United States. Rat baiting involved throwing rats to their doom by the hundreds. Pits, usually in the cellars of taverns, were dug and lined with tin to make it impossible for the rats to claw their way out. Sackfuls of rats were then added to the pits and dogs were allowed to chase and kill them. Spectators watched and egged the dogs on. They took bets on how many rats each dog could kill. The owner of the most bloodthirsty dog was declared the winner. The need for rats to fuel the sport became so great that rat catching became a profession.

Family Tree

All living things are grouped into different categories that describe things such as what an animal looks like and how they act. These groupings help scientists to figure out how different animals are related, and how they evolved over time.

Carl Linnaeus

Animals are identified and named according to a system of classification that was first developed over 300 years ago. The man who created this system is Carl Linnaeus, a nature-loving Swedish scientist. In 1738, Linnaeus published a book called *Systema Naturae*, in which he named and described many different species of plants. In the 1740s, he began classifying animals, too. His system of naming and describing living things is now known as taxonomy.

The system Carl Linnaeus set up has been altered over time to be more accurate.

Kingdom, Phylum, and class

Linnaeus's system grouped all living things into three different kingdoms. In the United States, most scientists now accept six different kingdoms of living things. They are: Animalia, Plantae, Fungi, Protista, Archaea, and Bacteria. These kingdoms are then divided into phyla, which describe basic body structures of a living thing. For example, worms and birds belong to different phyla because their bodies are designed differently. Living things are then broken up into smaller groupings, first by class, then by order, family, genus, and species.

Rodentia

Rats belong to a class of animals called Mammalia, which means that they are warm-blooded and give birth to live young, rather than lay eggs. The order Rodentia includes almost 2,300 different species. Rodentia includes rats, mice, squirrels, beavers, guinea pigs, voles, and porcupines.

Muridae and Rattus

Muridae is a family of mammals that includes rats, mice, and gerbils. It is the largest family of mammals, with about 600 different species. The genus Rattus includes about 300 different species of rats. There are only two species of commensal rats, or rats that live among people, *Rattus rattus* and *Rattus norvegicus*.

The only characteristic that all rodents have in common is that they have two long, sharp teeth called incisors. They use these teeth to bite, rip, and gnaw. Like rats, beavers are rodents.

Lab and pet rats

Albino, or white rats, are gentler, domesticated rats that are close relatives of *Rattus norvegicus*. Scientist Henry Donaldson first bred these rats in 1906. Dr. Donaldson wanted to create a species that could be kept in cages and would be less prone to biting handlers. It was important that these rats were standardized (all the same) to make experiments performed on them more accurate. Today, these tamer rats are also bred as pets. They have smaller brains, livers, kidneys, and other vital organs, including smaller adrenal glands, which are responsible for making wild animals feisty.

Lab rats were bred to be calm for life in cages.

Anatomy Lesson

Rats have two small, beady eyes. They can only see about four feet (1.2 meters) in front of them, but they can detect movement about 50 feet (15 meters) away. To make up for their poor eyesight, rats have heightened senses of smell, taste, touch, and hearing.

Thigmo-wha?

Thigmophilia, of course! This is a big word that means *the love of touching*, and rats are among the biggest thigmophilists in the world. They like to feel their way around things using their bodies. Rats' bodies are covered with thin, waterproof hairs that they brush along surfaces as they scurry from place to place. Their long, wiry whiskers help them detect things in their path, preventing them from bumping into walls in the depths of sewers and other dark places. Glands that are buried under the skin secrete oil, which they use to mark their territory and help them navigate familiar routes.

Flexible bones also make it easier for rats to survive blows and falls and still land on their feet.

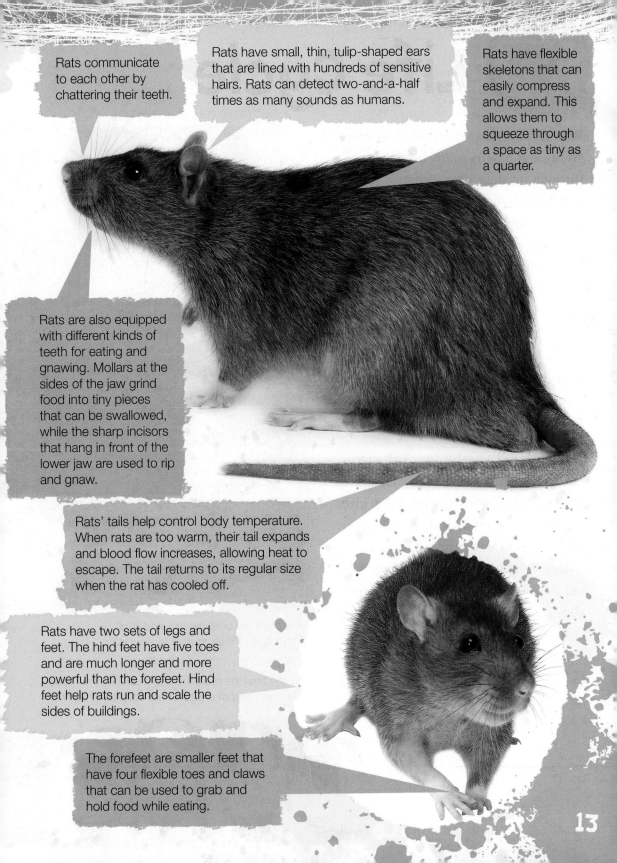

Rats communicate to each other by chattering their teeth.

Rats have small, thin, tulip-shaped ears that are lined with hundreds of sensitive hairs. Rats can detect two-and-a-half times as many sounds as humans.

Rats have flexible skeletons that can easily compress and expand. This allows them to squeeze through a space as tiny as a quarter.

Rats are also equipped with different kinds of teeth for eating and gnawing. Mollars at the sides of the jaw grind food into tiny pieces that can be swallowed, while the sharp incisors that hang in front of the lower jaw are used to rip and gnaw.

Rats' tails help control body temperature. When rats are too warm, their tail expands and blood flow increases, allowing heat to escape. The tail returns to its regular size when the rat has cooled off.

Rats have two sets of legs and feet. The hind feet have five toes and are much longer and more powerful than the forefeet. Hind feet help rats run and scale the sides of buildings.

The forefeet are smaller feet that have four flexible toes and claws that can be used to grab and hold food while eating.

Life Cycle

Rats are amazing reproducers, starting young and having many litters throughout their lives. Females, or does, are ready to mate when they are only 11 weeks old and have about 60 to 70 babies a year. Males, or bucks, have to wait a little longer because they grow more slowly in colonies where there are dominant, alpha rats. The bucks do not hang around after mating, but leave the doe to build a nest and prepare for her pups, or babies.

Rat's Nest

Females build a nest from cloth pieces, newspaper, and other soft materials. About 21 days after mating, a doe gives birth. Most litters include about seven pups, but some may be as large as twelve. After giving birth, the doe licks her pups clean. The pups are very tiny— about the size of a jelly bean. Their eyes and ears are sealed shut, so they cannot see or hear. They are also born without hair, so they must snuggle close to their mother to keep warm.

Rat pups are born hairless and must stay close to their mother for warmth.

By the time the pups are one week old, their eyes are open, and their bodies are covered in soft fur.

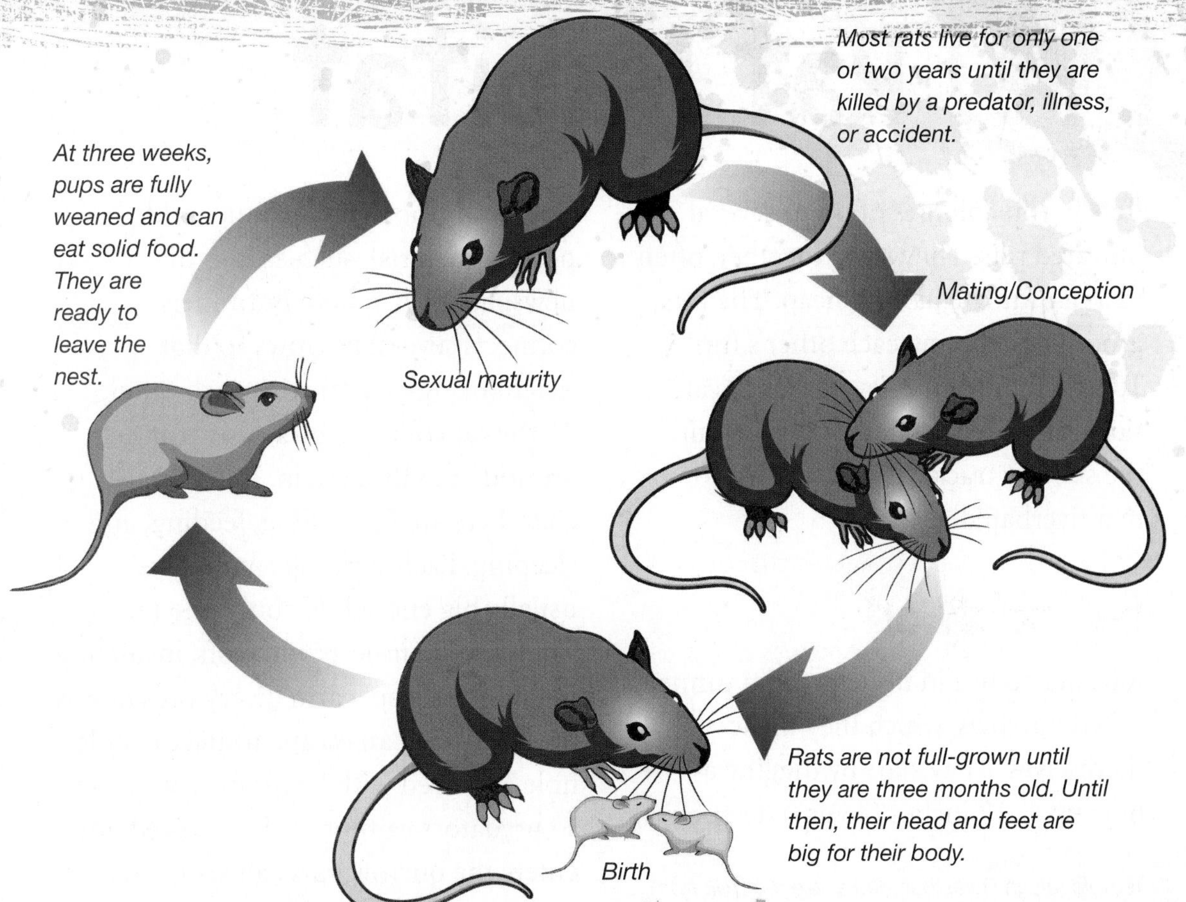

At three weeks, pups are fully weaned and can eat solid food. They are ready to leave the nest.

Sexual maturity

Most rats live for only one or two years until they are killed by a predator, illness, or accident.

Mating/Conception

Rats are not full-grown until they are three months old. Until then, their head and feet are big for their body.

Birth

That's creepy

Hairless Rats

The reason why there are so many species of rats is because they have so many babies, and because they do not have the same partners for life. Breeding with multiple partners allows for mutations in the gene pool. In other words, weird or interesting adaptations can happen in rats' biology that give them special characteristics. Hairless rats are the result of a gene mutation. These rats have no fur or whiskers. Hairless rats make excellent research subjects because they are prone to various cancers, and their lack of fur makes it easier for scientists to study tumors.

Rat Habitat

Rats live in colonies of up to several hundred rats. They sleep together, often in a pile known as a rat heap. The rats groom by nibbling each other's fur. Together, they find new places to eat, sleep, and breed, whether it is behind the subway tracks, under a house, or in a riverbank.

Hey, neighbor!

Rats like to live in underground tunnels, called burrows, which they make themselves. They start by digging a hole up to 18 inches (46 cm) deep.

Temple rats in Rajasthan, India, are fed milk from pans and are allowed the run of the temple.

They stuff the main chamber with nesting material, such as rags or newspapers. A system of tunnels connects several burrows so that neighboring rats can visit each other. As the rat colony grows, more tunnels are added to the system. Individual chambers are for nesting, feeding, and sleeping. Each sleeping chamber is usually big enough for only one rat. They line their nests with soft, insulating material to keep warm. Every rat's nest is designed with an escape route, or "bolt hole," covered with leaves or newspaper so predators cannot see it. If a predator enters the burrow, rats can scurry to safety out of their bolt holes.

Home Sweet Home

Rats are experts at finding homes. As long as they can find water and food, they can live just about anywhere: garden sheds, bird feeders, even garbage bins. They thrive in forests, warehouses, and shipping docks. They burrow under sidewalks and into office walls. In the desert, pack rats build their nests in cacti, which protect them from the harsh heat of the sun and cold nighttime temperatures. Rats mark their territory with their urine. Rat colonies have their own group smell, so rats from other colonies instantly know when they have reached the borders of enemy territory.

Australia 55
Stick-nest Rat
Endangered Species

The stick-nest rat, found on an island off the coast of Australia, makes a nest by piling sticks up to five feet (1.5 m) high.

crawly fact

Reincarnated Rats

Karni Mata temple in Rajasthan, India, is home to more than 4,000 rats. The Hindu worshipers who come to pray at the temple believe that the rats are the reincarnated souls of saints. Every night, ceremonial drums and bells sound as a priest presents a dish of rice to the rats. When the swarming rats have almost finished their meal, the priest retrieves the dish and passes it among the worshipers, who eat a few grains of rice each. The rats are thought to be so special that if a person accidentally steps on a rat and kills it, they must pay the rat's weight in gold or silver.

Pets or Pests?

It might seem hard to believe, but rats make excellent pets. They can live for up to seven years or more, can be trained to perform tricks, and never need to be taken for a walk!

Every Color Under the Sun

It is believed that pet rats came from breeding albino lab rats with wild Norway rats. This began around the mid-1800s, but very few people kept rats as pets at this time. The breeding of albinos with Norways led to some very interesting color variations, including shades of gray, brown, cream, chocolate, black, and even silver and blue. White belly patches and other interesting patterns also appeared in these domestic rats, as did hooded varieties.

In 1978, the Mouse and Rat Breeders Association was created in the U.S. Today, many people think rats are cool pets.

Rat Fancying

In a small English village in 1901, a woman named Mary Douglas began referring to herself as a rat "fancier." She insisted that the pet rats she kept in her home were far different from the wild rats that ran through the streets. Mary was so good at promoting rats as pets that the National Mouse Club changed its name to the National Rat and Mouse Club in 1912. In the United States, rats were not kept as pets until the 1960s, and even then, rats were by no means considered a "normal" pet.

Lab rats are used for research and experiments. Many animal rights activists are opposed to experimenting on animals, including rats, because the animals suffer before they are killed.

Under the Microscope

Many people wonder why lab rats are good research subjects. Their vital organs (brain, heart, liver, kidneys) work very similar to human organs. This makes rats the perfect candidates for studying diseases that affect humans, such as kidney and heart disease, Alzheimer's disease, and many forms of cancer.

Rats also respond to medications in the same way as humans, so new drugs are tested on rats before they are approved for humans. In addition, scientists can observe effects in rats only one or two years into an experiment; the same experiment performed on a human might take 70 years to observe.

Predators and Prey

When male rats meet, one usually crawls under the other, lifting the top rat right off the ground. It is a bit like shaking hands. If the rats are members of the same colony, the two rats continue to go about their business. But if one of the rats is a stranger to the colony, watch out!

Rat Attack!

Rats are not fierce animals, but they are very protective of their own territory. Males fight over territory, mating partners, and food. When a rat feels threatened, he arches his back and stretches his legs out, and his hair stands on end.

Rat Predators

Rats are a popular treat for many predators. In the wild, snakes, hawks, and foxes love to prey on rats. Cats, weasels, dogs, owls, and coyotes also prey on rats. Some rats are bred specifically for feeding to snakes and birds of prey at zoos. If food becomes very scarce in a rat colony, some rats may prey on and eat the younger, weaker members of the colony.

For snakes and wild dogs, rats are tasty meals.

Rat Prey

Rats are not real hunters, as they prefer to eat food scraps left behind by humans. They will eat the flesh of carrion, animals that are already dead. On riverbanks, rats will dig up earthworms and snails, removing the slimy treats from the shell. They will also eat small fish straight from the river. On farms, rats love to steal the eggs of chickens, and sometimes eat baby chicks. A very large, hungry rat may even kill an adult chicken.

Rats like easy meals, such as food left for livestock.

That's creepy

Rat plagues of Mizoram

Every 50 years, farmers in the Indian state of Mizoram prepare for a terrible rat infestation that can cause thousands of people to starve to death through famine. The trouble begins when the *Melocanna baccifera* plant, a rare species of bamboo, suddenly flowers and produces seeds. When the seeds drop to the ground, ravenous rats quickly devour them. This results in a population explosion. When the rats have eaten all of the *Melocanna baccifera* seeds, they turn to grain crops and storehouses, quickly eating through the food supply intended for the human population. In 2007, government officials in India tried to prevent another famine by offering people one rupee for every rat they killed.

You Dirty Rat

Rats have had a bad rap for centuries. In children's books, rats are often evil characters that steal from other animals and are always up to no good. A "rat's nest" describes a messy head of hair, and a "pack rat" is someone who never throws anything away.

I Smell a Rat

Rats run through the alleyways and infest dumpsters, but they have also made their way into everyday language. Rats have scurried into many common expressions, but rarely in a flattering way. "I smell a rat" means that something is wrong, while a person who is a "dirty rat" is a sneaky, wicked person. Betraying a friend is to "rat on" them. In classic Hollywood movies, a "rat fink" was someone who cut deals with sleazy mobsters and never thought twice about giving police the name of his boss.

Rats have a dirty reputation, but they do clean themselves.

We All Fall Down

In literature, rats are greedy, sometimes violent characters that cannot be trusted. In the children's classic, *Charlotte's Web*, Templeton the rat is a loner who despises the other animals for no reason. Even when the animals need his help, Templeton refuses until he is paid in edible garbage.

The plague, spread by rats, plays into the children's nursery rhyme "Ring around the rosy/ A pocket full of posies/Husha, husha/We all fall down." Although this rhyme was not actually written to describe the plague, it has come to be interpreted as such. Small bouquets of flowers, called posies, were said to ward off the disease. The word "husha" is sometimes replaced with "achew," meant to imitate sneezing, either from smelling flowers, or from being sick. The line "We all fall down" describes succumbing to the disease.

Pied Piper

Rats play an important role in *The Pied Piper of Hamelin*, a children's tale that has survived eight centuries. In the story, the town of Hamelin, Germany, becomes overrun by rats. A stranger in "pied" (multi-colored) clothing appears before the mayor of the town, claiming to be a professional rat catcher. The mayor grants the stranger permission to get rid of the rats any way he can. The stranger then charms the rats with music he plays on his pipe. The rats gather around his feet and follow as he marches them out of town. When the piper returns, the mayor refuses to pay him. The revenge-seeking piper leaves Hamelin, only to return wearing a disguise. Once again, he plays his pipe, this time luring all of the town's children away, never to return.

Rat Facts

Rats are both hated and loved wherever they go. Here are some rat facts that even the most murophobic—rat-fearing—person would have to admit are pretty cool.

A single rat sheds one million hairs each year. In the U.S., the Food and Drug Administration sets standards for the number of rat hairs that are safe for people to consume in processed foods, such as peanut butter and canned soup.

Rats cannot vomit, so they are doomed if they eat something poisonous. The reason they cannot vomit is that they have a muscular barrier between their esophagus, or feeding tube, and their stomach. Humans also have this barrier, which is what keeps food down. However, unlike humans, rats do not have strong enough muscles in their esophagus to open this barrier when something upsets their stomach.

Rats need to eat at least ten percent of their body weight every day. That adds up to 20 pounds (9 kg) of food each year.

Rats can hold their breath underwater for four minutes. They can enter a house by swimming up through an unused toilet.